Don't keep it to yourself

Don't keep it to yourself

Why you need to talk to make great software

by
Robert Drury
& Stuart Dawson

This edition published in the UK in 2018 by DKITY Limited.
info@dontkeepittoyourself.com

Copyright © DKITY Limited
All rights reserved

No part of this book may be reproduced in any form, or by any means, without prior permission in writing from the publisher.

For our families who make everything possible for us

Introduction	9
Overcoming the fear of speaking up	11
It's not just what you say	19
Exercises	24
It's tough talking to techies	25
Exercises	31
Considerations	31
Non-techies just don't get it	33
Exercises	37
Considerations	37
Don't keep knowledge to yourself	39
Don't let the team keep it to themselves	43
Recruiting communicators	49
Software leaders don't keep it to themselves	53
Acknowledgements	55
Further reading or listening	57
About the authors	59

Introduction

You must have sat in a meeting, listening to someone talk about the next great innovation and how it will revolutionise the way things are done. They've discovered the idea, the approach, or the improvement, that will take the business to the next level and they're enthusiastically extolling its virtues.

However, you've seen the flaw in their plan. The reason why all would not be rosy in the new world. It might be a minor thing or it could be major, but you know something that the presenter appears to have missed ... and you said nothing. You sat there silently, letting them carry on and didn't make a sound. Why did you do that?

There are many reasons why we don't speak up in situations like this, and in this book, we'll look at why this is the case, plus the challenges that businesses face when it comes to getting people to speak up, and why they must train and empower their teams to do more of it and do it better.

Unless you're extremely lucky, the only way to make great products is to have a team that are all pulling in the same direction. They need to know which direction it is that they should be pulling, what it is that they are pulling, and how hard they need to pull. To do that they need to communicate. Communicate the objectives, communicate the process, and communicate the issues. A failure to communicate will result in a virtually guaranteed failure of the task.

This book isn't intended to be a 'how to' book on a particular software development methodology, as there are plenty of books out there on Agile, Scrum and the like (some of which we'll list in the further reading section of this book). We do however touch upon occasions when you should be talking as well as how to talk effectively, and some of these are associated with certain approaches.

This book also isn't an instruction about how to go about talking to your customers, how to solicit feedback on your product, or how to sell your product. There are plenty of great books out there that focus on this area.

This book is a manifesto for not keeping it to yourself and for getting stuck in and talking with other people in your team. For individuals, it will help you overcome some of the worries that you may have when it comes to talking with others, as well as highlighting some of the areas where talking becomes a liability not a benefit.

We should also say that there are a few generalisations in this book, which are intended to help illustrate a point. We know that some software engineers are more eloquent than their non-technical colleagues, and vice-versa. We also use language such as 'techie' and non-techie' and we don't use it in a derogatory way. It's just shorthand language to identify two distinct groups of people who work within a software business. We also use the terms developer or engineer and they just mean someone of a more technical background, rather than making a genuine distinction between any kind of role.

Why have we bothered writing this book?   We've seen a lot of software teams over the years, and they could all have benefitted from more people willing to step up and talk things out, rather than keeping schtum. And because we've seen it a lot and have helped teams address it, we decided not to keep it to ourselves.

Rob & Stuart

Overcoming the fear of speaking up

"There's way too much fear in most organizations for actual communication to be possible."

Allen Holub, Principal, Holub Associates

The great American comedian Jerry Seinfeld is quoted as saying that "According to most studies, people's number one fear is public speaking. Number two is death. Death is number two. This means to the average person, if you go to a funeral, you're better off in the casket than doing the eulogy."

We can all understand this feeling as we've all felt the fear of having to stand up and talk in front of others at some point in our lives. Whether it's being asked to read Romeo & Juliet out loud in our English class at school, or those times when you go around the table to introduce yourself to a group of strangers in a business meeting and you need to say something interesting about yourself.

Sometimes it is difficult to speak in public, but the fear isn't just about standing up in front of a group and talking, but could be about a fear of having an opinion, a fear of being wrong, a fear of being seen as not very knowledgeable, or a fear of upsetting other people.

There could be a fear that saying the wrong thing might cost you your job, or might cost the business the next deal, or damage your relationship with your colleagues.

It could simply be the fear of muddling up your words and sounding silly, but, most people don't consider the reverse. What's the cost of not speaking up?

In 1980, in Damascus, Arkansas, Geoff Plum and David Powell, members of the US Air Force, were tasked with the maintenance of the Titan Missile. The Titan was the missile delivery system for a nuclear warhead, stored 15 stories underground, ready for deployment in the cold war.

The pair had entered the missile chamber one day to remove the dust cap from the missile, ahead of pumping in some liquid to help resolve a low-pressure problem that the missile was having.

Suited up like the men who come to take ET away, they realised that they didn't have the correct torque wrench to remove the dust cap.

They'd been delayed in getting in to the chamber, and because of the delay they didn't want to return the 15 stories to the surface to get the wrench, so they improvised.

They found a three-foot metal ratchet. The two parts to the ratchet didn't quite fit together but needing to push on with the maintenance they climbed aboard a hydraulic lift and raised themselves up the side of the missile with a nuclear warhead sitting on top, and started to remove the dust cap.

Each of the men were holding a part of the ratchet, and on completion of the job Plum hands the socket to Powell, and the socket falls through a small gap between the lift platform and the missile. The socket falls 70 feet, ricochets off a ring that the missile was sitting on and hits the side of the missile

The next thing the men know, rocket fuel is gushing out of the side of the rocket. This is rocket fuel that can explode quicker than you can look at it, and that can melt your skin if it touches you, so not to be messed with.

Sirens start blaring around the missile base as pressure gauges go crazy and warnings get triggered.

The control centre contacts Plum and Powell and ask what's going on and they describe the gushing rocket fuel, but do not come forth with the all-important cause of the leak.

The control centre needs to determine the cause in order to figure out what the plan of action is, but they're missing one important piece of information. The fact that there is a socket sized hole in the side of the rocket.

Minutes pass by as messages get passed up and down the chain of command, before the evacuation call is made, and an entire nuclear missile base is evacuated, leaving a nuclear missile left unguarded. Is there going to be a nuclear explosion in rural Arkansas?

Eventually guilt gets the better of him, and Powell comes forward with the all-important missing information, but it's too late. The two airmen sent back in to resolve the situation are stood outside the missile silo when it explodes, sending rocket, bunker and nuclear warheads up into the air.

One person died in the explosion and 21 were seriously injured as the entire launch complex was destroyed. It was a miracle that the warhead didn't detonate and was found in a ditch outside the perimeter of the base by an air crew search party. How different it could have been if Powell and Plum had simply come forward with the all-important information sooner.

Similar incidents of failing to speak up include, the Clapham Rail Disaster, where 35 people died after a rail inspector had not reported the loose wiring that caused the crash due to a fear of rocking the boat, or the case of Barings Bank in 1995 where senior managers didn't raise concerns about the high-risk trades that led to the collapse of the 200+ year old bank with losses of $1.3billion.

Now, we're not saying that not communicating in your organisation will result in such catastrophic outcomes, but, as we saw in the introduction, imagine that the proposed new approach to delivering something which has been adopted by the team might have a hidden overhead that no-one else has considered, but which you've identified. If you don't share your thoughts then the solution might get built without considering this downside, which could lead to problems down the line which could impact customers, or even your job.

Don't keep it to yourself

Or imagine you have a great idea for a new feature of your product. If you don't tell anyone this great idea then it won't get built, and if it doesn't get built then the business might miss out on a whole new revenue stream that could fund the growth that the business needs. And of course, you miss out on seeing your idea come to fruition.

Practice makes perfect

One place to start when overcoming 'the fear' is to prepare. Do your homework and know what you want to say, understand your subject matter, and prepare for the inevitable questions.

It doesn't matter whether it's a companywide presentation or suggesting a new feature to the product team, if you've done your research, know what you want to say, then you can get your story straight and take comfort in the knowledge that you know your stuff.

Preparation is everything and former Wales rugby international Richard Parks is someone who prepares, and prepares well.

In 2015 Richard was planning a solo, unsupported, expedition to the South Pole, where he was attempting to break the record for completing the task, which stood at an amazing 24 days.

The year before the attempt, Richard had already been to both the north and south poles, as well as climbed the highest peaks on each of the seven continents, in just seven months, but his Antarctic preparation was something else.

In need of fitness, mental and extremes training, in the nine months leading up to his expedition, Richard completed:

- The Yak Attack - a 400 km mountain bike race through the Himalaya up to an altitude of 5416m.
- The Jungle Ultra - a 230 km run through the Peruvian jungle, with temperatures of 40°C and 100% humidity
- The Brutal - a double ironman triathlon in Snowdonia in Wales, the double marathon of which involves running to the top of Mount Snowdon.

That's preparation!

You don't need to go to these extremes to prepare, but if Richard Parks can do all this to prepare for his challenge, surely you can find the opportunity to do a little bit of preparation, in order to meet your challenge?

If you know what you want to say then you'll have a greater opportunity to focus on how you're going to say it, as you won't need to think quite as much about what you're going to say. You free up some brain space to allow you to get your prepared message across.

Write up your notes, or even write up a script if you need to, so that you've got something to refer to as you talk. There's nothing wrong with having something to refer to. Stephen Fry isn't talking off the cuff when he presents the BAFTAs. He's got a teleprompter.

Make sure you have a focus for what the goal of your communication is. Do you want to give your opinion on something, happy in the knowledge that at least you've said something, or do you want someone to take a particular action based upon what you've said?

If you want someone else to take action, then define what those actions are so that you can refer to them as you progress. It could be getting the opinion from the Head of Marketing or sharing your cost savings ideas with the Finance Director, the important thing is knowing what you want to achieve and giving yourself an opportunity to do it.

There are, of course, occasions where you can't prepare in advance, such as an impromptu meeting that gets called and you're pulled in to give an opinion, but even in these scenarios you have the opportunity to make a valuable contribution, and don't forget, you've been asked to contribute so people want to hear from you.

One thing to be aware of is when your contribution is actually needed. Is your contribution needed in the meeting and after the meeting would be too late, or is there an opportunity to take away whatever has been directed to you and communicate back at another time? Just because you're being asked to contribute now doesn't mean that's when your contribution is really needed.

There might be an opportunity to review and consider the subject before feeding back, which gives you the time to prepare your contribution, however, it could also be a 'speak now and forever hold your peace' moment and you must contribute now.

Find out what your options are. Don't be afraid to ask. Understanding what's being asked of you will help in focusing you on what you need to do. It removes that 'do I or don't I say anything' feeling that we get in certain circumstances.

If you're asked to contribute now you'll need to do a bit of positive reinforcement of your own skills and abilities, because you've been asked to contribute as others believe you have valuable contributions to make. Chances are that they're not asking you out of politeness, but because they need something that you can give them.

You have skills and abilities and add value to the business, or else you'd have been fired by now! That's why you're there. To give your opinion.

With this reinforced sense of value, you should take a breath and give your opinion. Talk from your area of expertise, being honest and open, and if you're not sure then say so. Ask for clarifications, or more background information, and if you can't offer a valuable contribution then don't be afraid to say so (we'll say more about this later in the book).

Give yourself the best chance of adding value by finding out what value you're being asked to give.

Don't keep it to yourself

It's not all about talking

Of course, there are also more ways of getting a message across than just talking. We're not going to cover much about mime in this book, but many of the principles of good communication within these pages equally transfer to non-verbal media. Whether it's writing an email, or creating a presentation, clear and appropriate communication is essential in sharing your thoughts.

And that's an important point. Ultimately what you want to achieve is to get across a point of view from you to some other person or group of persons, and for that other person to understand what you've said so that they can use it to add value to what they do.

The method of communication should be the one best suited to both the audience and the message.

If you don't like talking to people and so send lots of emails, that's fine, but, there's no point doing so to someone who doesn't check their emails. They simply won't read what you've said.

If you need to convey a quite technical concept but the audience isn't overly technical then maybe a diagram will help put across the general principles, rather than a description with lots of technical jargon.

Always remember what your goal is and find a way to communicate this, and don't keep it to yourself.

Maybe an email is a soft first step to bring up your idea to a group that you're cautious about. Maybe a drawing on a whiteboard and a nudge in its direction might encourage some to start a dialogue with you that allows you to bring forward your suggestions.

I'm an imposter

Sometimes we don't speak up because we might feel like an imposter, who shouldn't really be saying these things. In which case, then this tale from, the best-selling graphic novel author Neil Gaiman might help.

"Some years ago, I was lucky enough to be invited to a gathering of great and good people: artists and scientists, writers and discoverers of things. And I felt that at any moment they would realise that I didn't qualify to be there, among these people who had really done things.

On my second or third night there, I was standing at the back of the hall, while musical entertainment happened, and I started talking to a very nice, polite, elderly gentleman about several things, including our shared first name. And then he pointed to the hall of people, and said words to the effect of, "I just look at all these people, and I think, what the heck am I doing here? They've made amazing things. I just went where I was sent."

And I said, "Yes. But you were the first man on the moon. I think that counts for something."

And I felt a bit better. Because if Neil Armstrong felt like an imposter, maybe everyone did."

Pulitzer Prize and Tony Award nominated writer Maya Angelou said "I have written eleven books, but each time I think 'Uh-oh, they're going to find out now. I've run a game on everybody and they're going to find me out."

We're all imposters.

We've all had that feeling. When we're due to speak in front of others and we think:

- What can I tell these people that they don't already know?
- I don't know everything about this subject, so how can I talk about it?
- What if something I say isn't right?

You feel like an imposter and you'll be found out. As such, you take steps to avoid being found out. You're definitely not alone.

The psychological phenomenon of Imposter Syndrome actually comes in a number of forms, and author Valerie Young, in her book "The Secret Thoughts of Successful Women: Why Capable People Suffer From the Imposter Syndrome and How to Thrive in Spite of It", has categorised them into five groups, which might help us understand what it is that we're going through and why.

Don't keep it to yourself

The groups are:

- The perfectionist
- The Superwoman / Superman
- The natural genius
- The rugged individualist
- The expert

The perfectionist
Do you have trouble delegating tasks to others because 'they never get done right'? Do you have this immense pressure to get everything right 100% of the time. If so, you're likely to be a perfectionist and as such, imposter syndrome is often close by. You set high goals and so when you fail you have a crisis of doubt, which leads thoughts of whether you should actually be in the position you are. You're an imposter.

The Superwoman or Superman
Do you find yourself working late at work, even though you've done your day's work, just to show you're still working? Do you want to work harder, faster, better than your colleagues to show people that you are worthy of your job title? You're trying to be super. It's not the work that's driving you on, but the recognition that you get from doing the work that you're craving. It is however often a false economy, as working too hard can have an impact on your ultimate performance, or even your health.

The natural genius
When you meet up with your family or friends, are you recognised as the smart one? Have you managed to be successful at pretty much everything you've ever done, without having to put in too much effort? You're a natural genius, but it's a double-edged sword. If you've had things 'come easy' all your life then it can really be a struggle when things all of a sudden don't follow the same script. Your reference point of being naturally good at things disappears, and you question yourself. You might even avoid situations where this might arise, so avoid new challenges.

The rugged individualist
Do you find yourself saying that you don't need anyone's help to get things done? Do you think the things you've achieved are down to you alone? This view where you as an individual is the source of all positive things can become your downfall. You see asking for help as being an admission of failure, rather than being a step towards success.

The expert
You're reading a job description and you meet 9 out of the 10 requirements, do you think you won't be able to do the job? Do you find yourself attending meetups, courses or webinars to give you that extra bit of information? You're trying to avoid gaps in your knowledge so that no-one can find you out.

Which imposter type are you?

The first step to doing anything about this issue is to acknowledge the areas where you suffer and be honest with yourself. By acknowledging it you will be in a position where you can take action and make forward steps.

Perfectionists need to be more forgiving of their mistakes, as they're a natural part of life. Maybe do less preparation so you know things aren't perfect.

Superwoman or Superman need to take recognition from their own views and not those of others. Criticism from others should be used to improve your performance, not to beat yourself up about.

Natural geniuses need to start doing things they're not great at and understanding that learning things is not a bad thing. You didn't naturally start walking and talking. You learned how to do it.

Individualists need to start accepting that they are part of a bigger thing, whatever it is. You're there because of what you did AND what others did, so keep involving others in what you do.

And experts, need to understand that asking others for help is not an admission of incompetence. You might even be able to share some of your expertise with them!

It's not just what you say

When it comes to any interaction, it doesn't just exist on its own. Each party comes to the relationship with their own experiences and expectations. They also come with different levels of communication skills, which can create challenging moments.

From his research, Neuroscientist Uri Hasson highlights that when the speaker and the listener really understand each other, their brains will actually behave in the same way, however, if they have different understandings or frames of reference, then the brains will behave differently. That is physically behaving differently.

The good news is that it is possible to learn how to get better at communicating.

In general terms, there are a few golden rules when it comes to communicating, which apply to all aspects of life, not just software development:

- Mind your body language
- Listen (and we mean *really* listen)
- Be open and honest
- Minimise emotion

Body language

When you walk into a room and look around seeking help, you're assessing how the people in the room are feeling. Are they happy or hostile? Which of them would you want to walk up to and start talking about a new feature idea or a broken web service?

It's amazing how we can figure this out without any words being said, but that's the power of body language. We learn over time how to pick up on subtle (and not so subtle) body movements, facial expressions, and postures, from which we can determine how people are feeling and what they're thinking.

From the defensive and closed looking person with their arms crossed, to the smiling open body shape of a happy approachable person, we start decoding a person's mood before we start talking to them, and we need to use this extra information in order to make the best use of our communication.

Should I speak to Dave, as he looks frustrated? Now might be a good time to talk to Jane as she seems happy and approachable.

Body language, including facial expressions, provides 55 percent of verbal communications.

Then when we get into conversation, we can also identify when there is a disconnect between what we see and what we hear, those mixed messages. "Yes, that's a good idea" is what we might hear but what we see is a turn of the head away from us and a look towards the floor. Do they really think it's a good idea or are they just saying that to avoid an awkward situation.

And of course, body language works both ways. As well as being able to read the body language of the person you're talking to, at the same time they're doing the same to you, so you need to consider things like your posture, gestures, eye contact, and tone, when you are trying to share your views.

Have you ever sat listening to someone making a presentation, and they're full of nerves, talking quietly and looking at the floor? Did you listen intently and fully believe what they're telling you? If they're not sounding convincing can they really convince you?

Dr Emily Grossman, an expert in molecular biology, broadcaster and educator, trains contestants for the FameLab International science communication competition and she says "Our brains contain 'mirror neurons' which automatically make us copy the emotions of the person we are engaging with. Have you ever noticed that if you see someone in the street smiling, you will start to smile too? If a speaker appears happy and relaxed, the audience will feel that way too, and will be more likely to absorb the information the speaker is trying to get across."

Some of the common signs of defensive body language, and therefore less approachable include:

- Limited facial expressions
- Minimal arm and hand movement, or crossed arms
- A body that isn't turned towards you
- Eyes that look down or away

When you begin to identify these signs, there is an opportunity for you to stop and consider what you're going to say and how you're going to say it. Just heading straight into the conversation when you can see that you'll receive a defensive response will likely result in an unsuccessful piece of communication, whereas by adjusting what and how you say it in order to make the recipient feel less defensive the more likely you are to have a favourable conversation.

This approach also applies when talking to groups of people. Have you ever been in a room where the audience are sitting quietly, arms folded and heads down, seemingly unengaged by the speaker? When you're the speaker it's your job to identify this, and adjust the way you're communicating to try and overcome this apparent disinterest.

It's not all bad though, as blank faces can be seen as listening faces, as people are processing what's being said to them. But there's a difference between blank and disengaged.

Don't keep it to yourself

Listening

One of the definitions of the word communication is 'the successful conveying or sharing of ideas and feelings', which is the meaning of communication that we're using here in this book. Someone talking to others in order to share ideas and feelings with a view to working together to deliver some great software, and one of the key words in this definition is 'successful'.

What makes the communication successful? The information relayed from one party to the other being understood, and in order to be understood the receiver needs to listen, and we mean *really* listen.

According to listening experts like Lyman Steil of the University of Minnesota, the average adult spends about 70 percent of his or her day in some form of communication. The most oft-cited statistics show that adults spend 9 percent of their communication time writing, 16 percent reading, 30 percent speaking and 45 percent listening. Therefore, if you want to improve your interpersonal communication skills, focus on becoming a better listener.

What's the point of communication between two parties if one party isn't really listening? Just being able to say that you've said something doesn't really cut it. It needs to be heard for it to be of use. When one party isn't listening, we can't really say that the communication is successful, because although one person might be speaking the other isn't really listening and so the point of the communication is being missed.

We can listen and hear the words, but if we don't really listen we might miss the tone, the bits between the lines, the feelings, or the real meaning behind what's being said.

In the sense of software development, does the project manager *really* want you to change the font to Gil Sans, or do they really want the flexibility for the end user to be able to change the font themselves? Do they really mean that they want the small code change to happen when you have got a minute, or do they really need it done sooner rather than later and they're just being polite in not trying to interrupt you?

If you're really listening then you'll spot some of the subtle clues in what's being said, and how it's being said, that will help you read between the lines and allow you to ask questions to clarify the real idea or feeling that's being communicated.

The better you are at spotting the clues, the better the chance of your communication being successful.

Emotions

Feeling passionately about something is a good thing. If you care enough then there's a greater chance you have of seeing something through. You believe in your business' desire to provide excellent customer care and it hurts you to think that the company has fallen short in some way. You really think that your solution is the best for the long-term success of the organisation, compared to the short termism view that others have.

This commitment is great when it's harnessed in the right way, although if the emotion escapes in other ways it can become detrimental to the goals you're hoping to achieve.

For example, you have a solution to a particular problem and have explained your solution to the group and how that over time it will be more efficient for the business. The group however says that although that would work that they want to pursue an alternative solution at this time because the alternative has more immediate returns for them. Standing up and arguing about how stupid the decision was, or how it isn't as a good a solution as yours, will most likely not change anyone's mind, but instead is more likely to antagonise the group and they may begin to think how difficult you are to work with.

It's the emotions that have sneaked out and lead to use of frustrated language and the questioning of the ability of others, which others won't take kindly to.

You need to remove the emotion from these conversations and stay focused on the shared goal that you have. You'll all need to work together to take the steps necessary to achieve the goal, and being a compassionate person who understands the viewpoint of others and doesn't fly off the handle when they might not get their own way, will go a long way to smoothing the path to success.

Honesty

Let's be honest. You've definitely been in a situation where you have been talking to someone and they are going on about something and you've thought to yourself 'that will never work' or 'so what?', however when asked what you thought you said, 'Sounds OK'?

Or, you've been involved in a status update meeting and instead of highlighting the delays you're experiencing because of a particularly challenging aspect of the work, you said that you're progressing well just to avoid any potentially awkward conversations or the thought of people thinking you're not very good at what you do.

Don't keep it to yourself!

It's this lack of honesty that could ultimately lead to problems further down the line that you could have helped avoid. And you're to blame! But when we're saying lack of honesty, we're not saying blatantly lying about things and saying black is white, and white is black. We mean being open and forthcoming, not hiding things that could materially influence how things will be approached in the future.

Telling someone that you will still be able to deliver a piece of code by the end of the day, when you know that you've still got a pretty large stumbling block to overcome, isn't being entirely honest and preparing others for the potential failure to meet the deadline.

Advising someone that the request they've made is fine, when you know that there will be some tweaks that will be needed down the line that you hope to address later, isn't going to help if the potential solutions won't meet the needs of the client.

Being able to be honest about areas of concern or potential failure will open up the communication to being more realistic, which is more well received as it becomes a real thing that can be handled, rather than a version of the truth that gives room for interpretation and therefore miscommunication.

It is definitely better to say now that something won't be delivered on time, than tell people at the time they were expecting it.

Would you prefer your mechanic to tell you that your car won't be ready as soon as he knows, so that you can make alternative transport arrangements, or when you turn up expecting to drive it away?

Exercises

Exercise 1
To prepare for those awkward introductions round a table, think of three interesting things about yourself that you can use. Try and think of one to do with work, one to do with your hobby or leisure activity, and one to do with something else.

Exercise 2
In your next meeting with anyone, be honest about everything you're asked, however uncomfortable it may seem. Give an opinion, tell them what you believe, and see what happens.

Exercise 3
Find an opportunity to speak in front of a group for five minutes. It could be a knowledge sharing lunch session, a demonstration of a new feature, or if you really want to push yourself an open mic comedy night. Just talk in front of others for five minutes

It's tough talking to techies

"They're so bloody self-opinionated and not always for the right reasons."

Martin Sjoorda, Entrepreneur

Let's start with the basics. Why do we need software developers? We want a solution to a problem, that is to be delivered via a mechanism that involves some kind of software programme. As software isn't written in standard spoken languages, but in coding languages, we need someone who speaks those languages.

If our solution needs to be something in German, we'd need to deal with German speakers. If it needs a medical solution you'd need someone fluent in the medical knowledge. It's just a fact.

Computer programs are complex things, with lots of parts which need to join together in order to make the magic happen.

Air traffic control systems, autopilots, self-driving cars, all the way down to the ability to buy this book on Amazon, they are programs full of code, written by software engineers which operate effectively the overwhelming majority of the time.

Because software is complex and has lots of interconnections, software engineers need to have logical minds that can conjure up ways in which we can get the right piece of data out of hundreds of millions of pieces of data, at just the right time, and show it to the right person, at the same time as thousands of other people are getting their right piece of data.

A failure of the software to do this correctly each and every time could have huge consequences.

"In software, intensive business areas companies might go bankrupt within a few days or even within a few hours if their software systems are out of operation."

Most software systems are not self-learning. Instead they are programmed to do specific things at specific times when given specific commands. It's the engineer's job to understand what needs to happen when and what triggers it, which requires a logical brain and a certain level of detailed understanding of what needs to happen.

Even a game as simple as Hangman has a number of logical steps which we as humans make without too much thought, but when that needs to be turned into software it leads into layers of conditional logic.

What happens if we guess a correct letter? We have to fill it into the blank spaces that the letter occupies. Then what? As people, we know what we need to do next, but the programme needs to be programmed to do the next thing.

It's this breaking down of the individual steps into a logical progression that can be followed by the programme that engineers excel at.

"I don't understand"

Three of the toughest words to say are 'I don't understand', but it's an important part of good communication to be able to say it when you feel it. Don't keep it to yourself!

There are times when you are in a conversation with an engineer and they get into the zone talking about the latest bit of code that they've written. They've managed to 'get the GetCustomer API responding in 0.5 milliseconds which means the view for the account renders better'. And you've started to glaze over because you don't understand the terms they're using and you have no idea why you should care about the speed of the API and what the view state is.

That's the point when instead of nodding politely, or starting to think of the next thing you want to do, you need to stop and say "I'm sorry, I don't understand what all that means. Can you explain it to me in non-technical terms please."

Really. That's what you should do, but you've probably not done this on many occasions.

Yes, you're showing you don't know something. Yes, you're admitting you're not perfect. But you know what, nobody is. In this scenario, the engineer also isn't perfect, because they've explained something in terms that only they understand which is a failure in their attempt to communicate to you, so you're no worse than them.

However, you have everything to gain. The engineer could explain their code to you again but this time tell you that it gets the customer's details much quicker than it did previously, which means the page the customer is waiting for will load with the right details quicker, which is a win for your customer. That's something you can do something with. You can talk about how as a business you're improving product performance, or there's been a 100% reduction in service response time. Benefits all round!

This is a relatively ordinary improvement, but the jargon that the engineer is talking could be about how they've found a new way to link X and Y together which opens up a whole new product area, or they've simplified the way that new releases of the product are done which means you can release features more regularly to your customers, or any other big positive leaps that impact upon your non-tech focused world.

You need to stop and find out what they really mean, or else you might miss out on an opportunity to make a big impact on your business, and all you have to do is say 'I don't understand'. Don't keep your ignorance to yourself.

In reality, if the engineer is so excited about the code then they will want to tell you about it anyway, so the chances are they'll be more than happy to talk about it some more. Who doesn't like telling someone how great they themselves are?

Question: When was the last time you said, "I don't understand"?

What do you need?

This section could easily have the subtitle of 'and why they should care'.

In our 2017 survey of software engineers, when asked, the overwhelmingly most important thing that helps them understand what it is that is being asked of them is receiving the underlying reasons for what is being asked. So not just what they need to do but why they need to do it.

It's not just I want a box for the user to write text in, it's a large box for the user to describe their work experience in.

It's not a copy of their invoice, it's the ability for the user to download any of the past two years invoices in a format they can read or email on to other people.

In the world of agile development, what you need from a techie would start out in the form of a User Story that would follow a particular format of who, what and why.

"As a bank customer,
I want to be alerted by text when my balance goes below £50,
so that I can avoid going overdrawn."

That's a pretty clear requirement, but, in addition to this, supporting information on the reason for the request are also beneficial. For example, "we've had 20 customers ask for this feature, and by analysing the occasions that customers go overdrawn we think that we can reduce the number of unintended overdrafts by 1,000 per month by giving the customers more information on the state of their account."

As well as this helping in understanding what's being asked, it also opens up the possibility of the engineer being able to use their expertise to suggest alternative solutions to the same problem which might not have been considered before. For example, "We already have the notifications function on the banking app. Could this be used rather than us sending a text message, as it might save some time?"

Think about when your partner asks you to do something at home such as 'Can you go and get me the box from the bedroom?'. Yes, you know they want the box from the bedroom, but you don't know why they want the box. You don't know why they can't just get it themselves. You don't know if there's something in the box that they think is there but you know isn't there.

You could turn away from this request resenting your partner for interrupting what you're doing to ask for something which you don't think is important. You could end up bringing down the box only for the thing your partner wanted to not be in the box and you knew that all along.

If your partner had asked 'Can you go and get me the box from the bedroom because I want to find the bank statement to balance the budget?' you'd understand that there is a budget to be balanced and that the statement will help do that, but you've also got the opportunity to suggest alternative solutions ("you can see the statement online from the iPad") or correct misunderstanding ("the statement isn't in the box. It's in the kitchen by the kettle."). It's the knowledge of the underlying reason for the request that allows for a satisfactory resolution to the situation to be found.

It doesn't take much more effort to give this extra information about the context of the request, but it could make the difference between the finding of a satisfactory solution and receiving a solution that doesn't meet the needs of the situation. Don't keep it to yourself!

On the other side of this, it also isn't hard for the recipient of the request to say, 'why do you need the box?'

Are you sure?

In addition to context, there are areas of requests where it's possible to provide more information to show that the idea has been thought through thoroughly, rather than just be an idea off the top of someone's head, which is another often stated bugbear of software engineers.

For example, if we return to the example of our alert to the bank customer when their balance gets low, before we spoke to the engineer we might have considered how many messages might we expect to send. This would be important for the development of services that can handle the right number of requests in a timely manner. We might have thought about whether there was any validation on the telephone number field to ensure the number is a correctly formatted mobile number which will allow a text message? Or what happens if the mobile number isn't in the country of operation?

All these things could be considered before approaching the software team, or else a product might get built that can only handle one text message a minute, or fails because the phone number isn't correct, or can't send a message to another country, or these questions get asked late in the day and risk the timescales for delivery. Or the software team simply refuse to talk to you because you've not got all the information they need to deal with the request.

You might not have the answers to the questions, but at least that gives the engineer a framework in which to get on with the task at hand, or highlight further areas for research BEFORE it even gets to the engineering team.

If we adjust our initial request to reflect this then our brief to the engineers might look something like this:

"As a bank customer,
I want to be alerted when my balance goes below £50,
so that I can avoid going overdrawn.

Followed by these criteria for assessing it:

Can the alert be received via text message?
Can the product send 60 messages per minute?
Can the customer enter their phone number in the form of 11 digits?
Does the customer get a message if the format of the phone number isn't correct?
Can the customer only set their country as the UK?"

Having this additional information shows to the engineer that the feature has been thought through, and it provides a framework for validating the story. Engineers can review the individual criteria and see what needs to be done, and they can ask questions around these individual points. Does it really need to send via text message or could we send a notification to the banking app? What do we plan to do with the customers we have that are based in Ireland?

The engineering team won't expect you to know all of the intricacies of the software, but they'll be expecting you to at least have considered as much as you reasonably could have done before you start talking to them. It goes from being a half-baked idea to a thought-out feature request.

If someone approaches you and says, "can you move that box?" your immediate response might be "move it yourself you lazy ****". Whereas if they'd asked, "Can you help me move that box because it's too heavy for me, there's no-one else around, and if it doesn't get moved then the wheelchair customer we've got coming in won't be able to get past" then you're likely to see what it needs moving for and why it needs you, and be more than willing to help to deliver a satisfactory resolution to the problem.

Is it really important?

A final area where engineers find frustrations is in the prioritisation of requests, or lack thereof.

Researchers at the University of California, have found that the average time lost when you are interrupted from a task is twenty-three minutes.

Given this, it's understandable that frustrations creep in if questions get asked at random points during the day, and once there are frustrations then the likelihood of a satisfactory outcome being achieved is vastly reduced.

Imagine you're halfway through writing the best presentation you've ever written, and every ten minutes someone comes to ask you where the stationery cupboard was, or what you did with the latest edition of a magazine. Or you're at home and painting a wall in the bedroom and every few minutes your partner pops their head round the door and asks your opinion on what to eat for dinner, or what they should wear when you go out in the evening.

In these instances, the things you're being interrupted with are important to the person making the request but they're not important to you because you're trying to focus on the presentation or the painting. On these occasions, the requester should consider whether this really is the best time to ask the question or whether it could wait until the presentation or painting is finished.

Just because it's important doesn't mean it's urgent.

Yes, there will be times when an interruption is required, because the thing you need to interrupt with is so urgent that it can't possibly wait, but the likelihood is that this isn't going to be the case on the vast majority of occasions.

To develop a good relationship with others you need to stop and ask yourself the question 'Does this really need to be prioritised ahead of what I'm doing and ahead of what the engineer is doing?'. If the answer is no, then make a note of it so that you can bring it up at a more appropriate moment.

When is more appropriate? Any time when it doesn't interrupt other work and before a decision is needed is fine.

It's Monday and if the answer to the question is needed by Friday, then Thursday is OK. If there's a deadline for a major client and the question relates to a nice to have future feature for a different client, then once the deadline has passed is fine.

Exercises

Exercise 1
Think about the last time you requested something from the engineer. Now think about how many questions they came back to you with in order for them to understand your requirements. How many of these questions could you have anticipated if you'd have thought about it long enough?

Exercise 2
Think about how many times you have interrupted an engineer this week to ask them a question. Now think how you might be able to group your questions together and have planned time with them in order to avoid repeated interruptions.

Considerations

How can you bring the intended outcome more to life for the engineer? It could be a mocked-up design or even a customer testimonial.

How can you show you've worked through all the scenarios that the engineer will need to create code for? It could be a flowchart or a list of possible outcomes.

How can you get to know more about the software from the development team? It could be a monthly show and tell session where they explain how something works, or it could be a repository of information on basic technical concepts.

How can you minimise the amount of interruptions you make to the engineering team? It could be a weekly meeting for all non-urgent questions or putting all questions in an email to be responded to at the end of the day.

Non-techies just don't get it

"The biggest challenge for engineers is convincing [non-engineers] that even though they just did a demonstration of the new stuff working perfectly, there is more critical work to be done before it can be released."

Eric Wadsworth, Software Engineer

Just stop for a minute and think about how many people work in your software business. Consider them all, from the guy on reception, to the girl in accounts, and that group of people on the first floor by the coffee machine.

Now consider what proportion of the people in your business are software engineers. Is it 25%? 40%? 60%? We can guarantee you it won't be anywhere near 100%.

Even if the business you work in is a software business, no business is purely made up of software engineers and all these other people have valuable contributions to make towards the success of the business and have skills required to play their part.

There are many on the technical side of software that think these people just get in the way. They mess up schedules, interrupt coding, enforce pointless administration tasks (yes, it's a generalisation).

These non-techie folks know about depreciation, social media, or bank transfers. They know about legal requirements, how to schmooze a client, or what to arrange for a sales event. As Bill Nye, the science guy says, "Everyone you ever meet knows something you don't".

All these skills are required in order to work towards the success of the business. There's no point writing some killer code if nobody ever uses it because nobody has sold it. There's no point working late to get the latest feature released if there's nobody around to process your salary payments and you don't get paid. Someone has to make sure you've got a room in which to work, hardware on which to code, and money with which to get paid.

They're valuable contributors to the success of the business, and just because they don't write software, understand C# or Python, or have ever built a website, doesn't mean that they're less valuable to the business than the software engineers.

From the other side of the fence, many non-techies in software businesses feel as if they're an inconvenience whenever they go to talk to an engineer, but they have their roles to play in the business and sometimes this will cross into the world of the engineer. Their requests will be important to the business, although they may not appear to be completely relevant to the engineering team.

Why should I fill in this form about the hardware I have? Why do I need to sit through a video on data protection? Why do I have to spend an hour listening to the HR person talking about pensions and health and safety?

These examples are all things that are required as part of the operation of the business and are as much a part of the job of a software engineer as writing new code. They will help the business save money, avoid legal cases, or support you in the long term as well as meet legal obligations.

Explaining tech concepts

"Creating an understanding in the non-tech team of just how much documentation and testing is involved in just a few code changes is a real challenge."
Ned Boff, Software Engineer

'The problem with them is they just don't understand' is a common phrase that has been heard in nearly every software business, and it's usually directed from the engineering team towards the non-technical parts of the business.

They don't understand the complexities of the system that exists, or the interdependencies, or the time it takes to test things in all its possible permutations and across the numerous devices and operating systems.

But can you blame them for not understanding, something they've not studied and which isn't part of their job? They need help in understanding and there's only one place this help can come from. Those who understand.

Our brains make sense of the world by constructing meaning from the information around it, and one way it does this is by connecting information about something it already knows to the new concept that it is trying to understand to make life easier.

We all do it and we've been doing it since we were children, and if you've got children then chances are that you already understand this approach because you're constantly doing it with your little ones.

"You're nearly right darling. That's not a duck it's a swan.
It's like a duck because it is a bird and swims in water, but it's a bit bigger and it's white"

Through this reference to something that's already understood we can help someone who doesn't understand the concept to make some mental leaps to get closer to what it is that we are trying to explain.

In software terms, examples could be:

- Databases as storage boxes
- API requests as questions

- Scheduled tasks as calendar reminders

We could describe something in this way:

The Alberto Service calls the GetUserData service so we can put the user's transaction log in the history view

However, this approach relies on the non-techie understanding the meaning of 'The Albert Service", "GetUserData Service", 'Transaction logs" and "History View" in order to understand how this process works. Alternatively, we could say:

We have something which asks another system for a set of information about the different purchases that the customer has made, and it gives us back the information so we can put it on the screen for the user to see.

It means the same thing, but can be understood on a satisfactory level by the recipient of the information regardless of their technical competency.

It's not dumbing down. It's finding an appropriate level of understanding and it's something we all benefit from when it's done for us in areas of our lives where we're not experts.

When asked how big metal cruise liners float and don't just sink to the bottom of the ocean, you don't dive straight into Archimedes Principles, but instead talk about the size of the boat compared to the water it pushes out of the way.

Speak simply

Finding that comparative framework makes that understanding for the non-techie much easier, which in turn makes the job of the techie much easier; win- win. There are no prizes for the amount of technical jargon you can use in a sentence, only for making progress as a team.

There might be a culture in your business where appearing as an expert is highly regarded, however, if you only appear as an expert by those who understand all the ins and outs of the technology that you use then you run the risk that a large proportion of your business won't know about your expertise, and they don't get to share in your knowledge.

Sure, if you know about server performance, are a React guru, or can tame Python better than the next person, then you'll likely have some respect from your boss and your colleagues.

But if the product manager knows what you're good at and you make them feel like they understand the technology, then who might that product manager turn to when they have a new idea they want to pursue?

If you can explain to the sales team how a new piece of breakthrough technology really works then they'll be able to walk into the boardroom of a potential new client and hold their own when it comes to the technicalities and win an exciting new project that utilises the cool tech, thanks to you!

Sharing knowledge in a clear way will lead to greater opportunities for both the business and for the individuals involved.

One business that had a considerable amount of client transactional data, faced the problem that the more clients they had the slower the reporting systems became and they needed a solution to be found. The solution had to allow this data to be quickly accessible, flexible in how it was accessed, and for it to have large queries made upon it, with no impact on service performance.

The solution entailed the transfer of data out of the place where it was gathered into a separate system, and into a different format. The tech team could have waffled on about ETLs, which mean nothing to non-techies, or they could explain the need to extract the data, transform it into a better format, which would allow it to be loaded more effectively. Extract, transform, and load: ETL.

Exercises

Exercise 1
Think of a concept related to the way your software operates. It could be how you go about deploying new releases or how you transfer data from storage to the screen for the customer. Now write a description of this so that it is no more than 200 words. Don't cheat and use acronyms! Now re-write the description and remove any of the technical words that might have crept in, replacing them with everyday words.

Exercise 2
Following on from this, think of how you can share this information with the team so that they can use it in their role to move the business forward.

Exercise 3
Visit http://splasho.com/upgoer5/ and try and explain a technical concept only using the thousand most frequently used English words. It's quite tricky given the technical nature of software, but it helps you in trying to think of alternative words for things.

Considerations

How can you improve the understanding of technical concepts to your teams? It could be diagrams or lunchtime talks.

How can you help others understand the technical terminology in everyday use in your business? It could be an accessible glossary or a weekly email containing definitions of new terms.

How can you brief a non-techie on the outcome of some research or investigation so that they know the impact upon things in their world? It could be confirming numbers of customers affected or anticipated downtime for end users.

Don't keep knowledge to yourself

"It is with words as with sunbeams. The more they are condensed, the deeper they burn."

Robert Southey

When you start a new job, one of the first things you need to do is get some of the knowledge that has built up in the business into your head, so that you're able to get on with your job.

If you don't know how things work it will take you a lot longer to figure out what needs doing. One shortcut to obtaining this knowledge is asking someone, but a) that might cause lots of interruptions, and b) the person you need to ask might not work there anymore.

That's where the power of documentation comes in.

In addition, it's also not just a benefit from a good piece of documentation, but as author Andy Wootton says, "It's easy to forget that an important part of communication is the knowledge you pass on to your future self". Being able to refer to your previous decisions, or your step-by-step processes again and again, will make future activities easier.

When should I document something?

There are three main areas that we consider it important to document things and not keep to yourself.

Features
As you work your way through the list of requirements and deliver new features to your customers, it is important to track these somewhere. As always, nothing too detailed, essentially all that needs to be covered is:

- What does the feature do?
- Why are we delivering this feature?
- How will the feature be managed and updated?

- Any other details or information that might be relevant

Complex Areas
As much as you should always strive for simplicity, inevitably some parts of what you're delivering will have to be complex. These can generally be identified as they are hard to explain verbally and will often require drawing a diagram and some explanation ... and that is all you need, a diagram or two and a little bit of context; What does this do? Why is it needed? How does it link to other elements? Are there historical reasons for why this works in the way it does? What does the diagram describe?

Repeatable Tasks
As your team grows and new members join they are going to require a period of ramp up time. Not only will they start off slowly, helping them get up to speed will slow *you* down as well, so one way to avoid unnecessary slowdown is to write short, succinct How To Guides for any repeatable tasks. Good candidates for this might be:

- Setting up a new copy of something that already exists
- Completing action A which will happen on a periodic basis
- Getting data from one place to another

In short, if more than one person is going to need to know how to do something, there should probably be a How To Guide for it.

What does a good piece of documentation look like?

Documentation has a habit of going out of date quickly, so the general rule is that if it is difficult to maintain, then it won't be maintained. To be honest, even if it isn't difficult to maintain then it is very easy to forget about maintaining it anyway!

That's why the best documentation is very often short and succinct. So, keep your documentation to the point.

A How To Guide, for example should simply cover the following as succinctly as possible:

- What is the task?
- Why would one perform it?
- Steps to perform it

Sometimes the work we're doing is investing a subject and working out how something might work in the future. For example, how should we go about introducing new feature X, considering that we already have features Y and Z which it will need to work alongside.

Don't keep it to yourself

Documenting the results of this kind of research is an area that often ends up with too detailed, or too vague, an output. This is often down to the fact that the outcome of the research was not clearly enough defined in the first place.

If you're defining a research task, it's very easy to get caught up in waffle, but what is required can be broken down clearly by following the points below:

- What is the outcome of the task?
- Context to why this is being asked (optional)
- List the questions that need answering

Diagrams are always helpful, particularly when describing your features that might involve numerous parts, or steps, or systems. If diagrams are too complex, they are gibberish to anyone that is not technical. Conversely, if they aren't detailed enough they are pretty useless to those who are trying to understand how things will ultimately be built.

One potential framework for communicating on different levels is Simon Brown's C4 model, which developed out of system architecture. In this framework, the model is based around having different diagrams focused on different views of the same element. The collective diagrams mean you have everything from a big picture down to a zoomed in view.

The C4 model is made up of four Cs:

System Context diagram
This is your big picture diagram. You draw a box in the middle which represents your system and outside of it you add all of the systems and users that interact with your system.

For developers, this might cover databases and third-party systems, whereas for non-developers this might be website pages.

Container diagram
This is where you step one level down by opening the box that represents your system and looking inside. You still see the other systems that interact with yours on the outside of the box but inside your system box you see containers that represent all the different parts within your system, at a high level.

For developers, a "container" is something like a web application, mobile app, database, file system, etc. essentially, a container is a separately deployable unit that executes code or stores data. For non-techies, this could be the different elements on the website pages, such as headers, footers, navigation, main content area etc....

Component diagram
Stepping down another level, you produce Component diagrams to look inside each container, showing how a container is made up of a number of "components" and what each of those components are.

For developers, this would look at the technology and the implementation details of the component, whereas for a non-developer it could be the different fields on a contact form and the data its collecting.

Code diagram

The final step is to drop down to the code level for each component, which is optional and most relevant for developers who can use UML, Entity Relationship Diagrams or similar.

And that is it. The collection of diagrams work hand-in-hand to give a high-level overview of your system to a range of people.

Don't let the team keep it to themselves

A key part of Agile development is the sprint retrospective, because it is fundamental to the process of continuous improvement. However, the idea of a retrospective can be useful, regardless of the development methodology that you follow.

Generally, it's a chance to look back at the recent work you've been doing, talk about what went well, what didn't go so well and how we can do things better next time. Project reviews that happen in Waterfall methodology to do the same.

There are many different styles of retrospective and in fact there is a great site, funretrospectives.com, which actually categorises retrospectives for different occasions, however, the key to running any retrospective is to get people talking about the things that matter the most to them and how they can help improve the work being done.

Successes and Challenges

This is a standard, "go to" retro, which is used in many agile businesses, and all you need are post-it notes (preferably in two different colours; one for "good" and one for "bad"), somewhere to stick them and somewhere to log any actions.

At the start, the post-its are scattered on the table and team consider what went well in the time since the last retrospective ("good") and what didn't go so well ("bad") and write short comments on the notes to represent these ideas. The post-its are then stuck to the wall, "good" together and "bad" together and potentially grouped within this if they appear to relate to one another.

The facilitator then introduces each note in turn, starting with bad usually (it's good to end on a high!) and gets the person that wrote it to expand. One of several things then happens here:

- A discussion opens up, often starting as a "Doing X has really hacked me off" and then through respectful questioning and probing, the team can get to the root cause of the problem, identify if there is anything that can be done to avoid it and if so, log the next action to take to achieve this.
- The subject has already been covered and hence you move on quickly
- It was just quick point (bad or good, or sometimes just highlighting how well another team member did with something) and there are no next actions to log.

An allowance of an hour for this is usually fine, but sometimes it can take a little longer. If you are pushed for time and have a lot of post-its to cover, you might want to consider letting the team vote for their most wanted topics by allowing them each to go up and add ticks to 5 post-its. The top X post-its then get covered in the session.

It's an amazing feeling introducing retrospectives for a team that feel they aren't really working well and seeing over time the number of bad coloured post-its reducing and the good coloured post-its increasing. It's a great visual representation of progress and an opportunity to point out how the team are affecting their own performance and making changes for the better.

The Focused Retrospective

When there is a particular issue that needs attention, this retrospective can really help dive down into the detail and get to the bottom of the issues and find out ways to make improvements. All you really need is a whiteboard and some pens.

Start the session by explaining the problem, for example, "we've missed our goal three times in a row" and then get the team to call out all of the issues, large or small, that have contributed to the problem. Once the list is in place, talk through each point with the team and build a list of actions that can help overcome these issues.

Once the list of actions is in place, get the team to vote (by allowing them 3 ticks to put against actions) for the actions they feel are most important to address and once you have these, get them into the backlog to make the work happen.

Two heads are better than one, so sharing thoughts in this way can make a huge difference to resolving major problems before it's too late. Of course, agreed resolutions also hold more sway than imposed ones!

Hopes & Concerns

In times of change or uncertainty, such as potential takeovers or the opposite, layoffs, this is always a good retrospective to run to unite the team.

First, draw a vertical line on a whiteboard. Then, on the left side, write the title "Hopes" and on the right, "Concerns".

Once this is in place, explain to the team the reason for the exercise, for example, "As we all know, our company is being acquired by Acme Inc in March and with this will bring a lot of change. As this is an unsettling time, I'd like to a run a different sort of retrospective today to discuss our hopes and concerns.".

Now dish out post-its and get the team writing and sticking them in the appropriate column on the board.

As with the Successes and Challenges retrospective, once all notes are on the board, see if you can group any and then begin walking through each one, getting the person who wrote it to expand upon their post-it headline.

The great thing about this exercise Is it gets things out in the open, people can discuss what is on their mind and - as they say - a problem shared is a problem halved.

There's no point ACME Inc buying a business with a disheartened team, and if the team have lost their motivation due to the uncertainty of redundancies, leaving it unaddressed might make the business situation worse.

Gauging Team Mood

At the end of a retrospective, another idea is to get a rough gauge of the general mood of the team. There are many ways to do this but two quick exercises are; Fist of five, and Word before you go.

Fist of five
This is very simple. Everyone holds out their fist. On the count of three, every holds up between one and five fingers. One finger indicates being very unhappy and five being very happy.

Take an average at this point to be the rating for the general feeling, and you'll soon get a feel for the team mood, however, if someone is quite different to this, it's a good chance to ask them why they're not in step with the others. Sometimes people just like to be asked.

A word before you go
Another simple exercise, again using good old post-it notes.

At the end of the retrospective, get each team member to take a post-it and write one word on it to describe how they feel at this moment then stick it to the wall.

Once everyone is done it can be good to review the words quickly, particularly any strange ones!

This can be quite uplifting, the more positive one's teammates are, the more it might brighten you up and write something more positive than you might have.

Contributions

Of course, with all of these retrospectives it's important for the team to contribute their feelings and thoughts and not keep them to themselves.

The only way to affect change is to be honest and share thoughts, respectfully, and make non-judgemental suggestions for ways to improve.

Don't let the same characters hog the discussion. You must get everyone involved, which is the role of the facilitator, and that is where some of the thoughts from earlier in the book come in handy.

These days there are many apps that do similar things, sending out prompts for feedback on everything from the general mood to how regularly you want to hear from the big boss, but sometimes the personal touch adds much more value.

Take time to talk: one to ones

For managers, part of their job is to keep their team happy as well as high performing. This means listening! As discussed earlier, the retrospective is a core place to do this, take in what's been vocalised and take constructive steps to address any issues.

You might think that having spent an hour every couple of weeks hearing what people have to say and working on ways forward, that that would be enough. If that is your view, we'd say you were missing something. Some of the best feedback and ideas come from one to ones with individual team members.

Just arranging a regular 20-minute chat over a coffee once every couple of weeks provides a chance to:

Get to know a little about your team member and connect with your team. Share a little about yourself and vice versa. Are they having issues in their personal life that might affect their mood at work? Perhaps they are trying to buy a house and will need time to meet with mortgage advisors, or their baby is ill and sleep is a challenge. The more you know about your team, the more you can understand and support them when they need it.

Gather feedback that the team member might not have felt they could share in a group. Maybe there is something that you or the team are doing that could be done better but your team member doesn't feel comfortable raising in front of the group for fear of being shot down. And maybe they are right! Better to get the feedback somehow.

Discuss ways of dealing with a difficult team member. Inevitably in teams you are going to get personality clashes at times and although they can often resolve themselves, sometimes things can build up and the one to one is great opportunity to find out about any such issues and from that work out how to deal with them.

Don't keep it to yourself

Find out about an interesting external activity that could be really beneficial to attend. More often than not, it is during a one to one that one of my team has mentioned an upcoming meet up or conference that is highly relevant to the whole team. From taking the time to find this out we can then book in the time to attend, whereas without informal chat the team member might not have felt confident enough to recommend it to all.

Get suggestions that didn't get heard in the retrospective. Way back, one of the team (thank you, Faesel!) raised the idea of using a physical board to track work as well as the online board and we agreed to give it a go. Since then, we've never operated without one! You can't beat them, if you haven't tried this, give it a go!

Address performance issues early. Having a regular catch-up is not only a platform for all the nice stuff, it's also a chance to address any performance issues early, before they grow. If a particular team member is not giving others a chance to speak during meetings, you might want to make them aware of this. If someone is "conveniently" avoiding core tasks, again, another chance to make them aware. Having these early, informal chats can halt a lot of problems before they've barely begun.

The key to one to one conversations is to make them relaxed and informal. If you can pop out for a coffee all the better, as different environments help lead to different mind-sets. They will also depend on the person that you are having the one to one with, different people have different needs. Some people just like a quick functional check in, while others prefer to spend slightly longer and desire feedback on how they are performing and how they might improve. There are no hard and fast rules. Just have a basic format and play the rest by ear. But make sure you do them!

Yes, it's easier if the team is smaller, so you might need to adjust the frequency if the team size is a little larger, but it shouldn't stop you doing them. Being proactive takes less time than being reactive.

When things go wrong: 5 Whys

Despite the best efforts of the team, sometimes things will go wrong. It's happened in every business we've worked in.

For example, an important report has been incorrectly calculating one of its figures for the last six weeks. The website of your biggest client was unavailable for two hours during a key time, or the daily data transfer didn't happen and now everything is out of date and processes can't run. Oh no!

These things happen, what is important is that we learn from them and - in the spirit of continuous improvement - put in place measures to prevent us from repeating the same mistake again.

A good way of getting to the root cause of the issue and then actioning ways to prevent it in the future is to run a 5 Whys session with the team.

Put simply, you start with what happened and then repeatedly ask "Why?" until you get down to what really caused it to happen. Once you know this, you can agree how you will prevent it from happening again.

The "5" part is in the title as this is observed as generally the optimum number of "Why?"s required to reach the root cause. This is not always the case though, sometimes it can take fewer or greater attempts than 5.

The outcome of the session can also depend upon the experience and perspective of the people in the room doing the questioning and answering and not all problems have a single root cause. To uncover multiple root causes, the method can be repeated asking a different sequence of questions each time.

Sometimes the answer to a "Why?" may lead to fork in the line of questioning at which point you'll want to take the questioning down each branch of the fork. This too can lead to multiple root causes.

As we say, running a 5 whys session with different groups may result in different outcomes but almost always, what comes out of a session will be solid, productive steps to stop the same problem recurring.

As with all of these team discussions, the key to their success is the ability of the team to share their thoughts with the group. There's no point doing the exercise and only one or two people contribute, as that limits the experience being accessed in order to find the cause and suggest a solution. You might not get the right cause and therefore you won't get the right solution.

Recruiting communicators

"If you think it's expensive to hire a professional, wait until you hire an amateur."

Red Adair

For those who are responsible for hiring new team members, it is imperative for you to find members of the team who already understand the challenges highlighted in this book and know some of the ways to overcome them it is going to be key to the ongoing success of your business.

If you don't hire them then you'll have to train them, and that takes time and money.

If you've spent time developing a team that works based on trust and communication, and you then hire someone who's not as comfortable talking openly, then there's going to be some bumps along the road as the different approaches come up against each.

It might be that the new employee doesn't feel confident to speak up, or they're used to being protected from product stakeholders and remain comfortable in a world where they can talk techie and no-one minds. However, if their new team are used to hearing opinions and encourage participation from product owners and business leaders, then you might find an unhappy employee, or at the very least one who isn't contributing all they can to the business.

The question is, how do you know if the interviewee has the communication skills that you're looking to utilise in the business.?

If you want to know if a JavaScript developer can make an automatically updating time and date widget, then give them a task of creating a widget. If you want to know if a product manager knows about KPIs, then test them on their own product's KPIs.

So, if you want to know about their communication skills then the thing to do is ask them to communicate something.

We're often quite ready to give role specific skills tests to people during an interview process, but we appear more reluctant to test on some of the softer skills that we need to find in our potential colleagues. However, given the importance of communication to organisational success it's just as important as any technical skills a potential employee might have.

Testing for communicators

Much of this book has covered the types of skills needed to be a good communicator, so the testing is simply a mechanism for bringing these skills to the fore.

For engineers, there are opportunities for them to explain a technical concept to a non-technical person as part of the interview process. This could be in person or written but at the end you'll know if the non-techie understands what was being discussed. You can make it about the candidate's existing codebase so they are the experts and the non-techie in your business won't be starting from a point of knowledge.

To test the level of understanding that the non-techie has gained, you could get the interviewee to write both a technical and non-technical version, so that you can ask questions of the non-techie and see what they've learned, or ask the non-techie to determine some follow up questions and you can gauge the level of understanding from that.,

There's a podcast called David Baddiel Tries to Understand, which follows this approach, where comedian David Baddiel chooses a subject that he doesn't understand, from suggestions made by members of the public. It might be Bitcoin, Fracking, or Pi, and he gets domain experts to explain the concepts to him. At the end of his research, his task is to explain the concept back to the original suggestor of the topic, as well as the expert he has gathered the knowledge from, in the hope that he now understands the basics enough to be able to explain it.

Does the engineer use technical language and specific terminology that wouldn't be understood by someone outside of the business or outside of a technical role? Does the engineer manage to strike a balance between too much and too little information?

From the other side, for those who interact with software engineers regularly then there are opportunities for them to describe a new requirement that they have to a technical person, and see whether the technical person is clear on what's required and why it's required.

You could ask them to write a briefing document and then to talk the engineers through it, paying attention to the terminology they use, assessing whether they reference how it interacts with other aspects of the product or why the request has come about.

Then there's the need to test for open and honest feedback. You could ask them for their thoughts on the original job advert or job description relating to the role they've applied for, or to critique your own product, but that might be a bit daunting in an interview, so maybe getting them to critique their own products and suggest areas for improvement would help show if they're someone who likes to moan, or someone who thinks things through and has constructive feedback.

Sample interview questions

Don't keep it to yourself

For engineers

- Tell us about the last feature that you worked on and how it operates.
- Describe the concept of APIs to us, with the assumption that we are not technically literate
- Write a requirement document that needs to be reviewed and prioritised by the Product Owner, and which relates to the need to address a security problem that has been identified relating to customer data.
- What are your top 3 priorities for next week?

For non-engineers

- Tell us about the last feature you had released, why this was released, and how it works
- Describe the concept of a product roadmap and why it's important
- Write a requirement document that needs to be reviewed by an engineer, and which relates to the sending of a notification to a customer when their account is going to be deactivated
- What are your top 3 priorities for next week?

Software leaders don't keep it to themselves

As part of the research for this book, we've spoken to a number of individuals from software businesses about how communication, or the lack of it, has impacted their businesses.

We looked to understand the challenges they faced with communication within teams and across teams, as well as finding out when communications failed and their business was negatively impacted.

Below, we've included some of their top pieces of advice when it comes to communication.

Bruno Suarez Laffargue, Head of Delivery, Just Eat

"When it comes to communicating, be brief, be bright and be gone."

Fergal O'Connor, Global Head of Software Development, Innovation Group

"At every opportunity make sure you repeat over and over again what you are trying to communicate"

Ole Dallerup, Senior Vice President of Engineering, Trustpilot

"My top tips for getting teams communicating together are: Set clear ownership and direction; Setup an environment that encourages people to talk together; Give teams the same measurable goals."

Steve Morin, Chief Technology Officer, Tripping.com

"Kick off meetings are a must, setting out points of contact and areas of responsibilities, so people know who is doing what."

Cheryl Bromander, Innovation Consultant in the Healthcare & MedTech industry

"There is no magic book. Understate all disciplines AND be willing to educate many stakeholders on why things are being done."

Eric Gilbert, Product owner at Harris

"The best piece of advice I've had on how to communicate is that you should be honest, and have no filter. Nobody's getting hurt!"

Adrian Lander, Agile Transformation Coach, Executive Business Coach and CEO of a consultancy

"In non-technical team's challenges are trust, openness, and hierarchy. In technical teams the challenges are communication through tools (like JIRA) instead of face to face, and a lack of support of good communication tools to support distributed teams. As such, you should move away from task communication to communication on work in progress activities, communicating what does not go well and the exceptions."

Acknowledgements

Between the two of us we're approaching forty years of working in the software industry, alongside a lot of people who have given us the experience that has enabled this book to be written.

Some of these folks have made our lives easier and some folk have made it harder, but both sets have helped us develop our own skills in communication and team building, and given us the opportunity to not keep it to ourselves.

Given what we've just said about some people making life harder we won't be naming names, but if you're one of the people from our previous lives then you'll probably know which side you were on, but thank you either way!

We also need to acknowledge the efforts of our families who have to listen to us at the end of the day when we bring our day job home. The times they've had to listen to the challenges of trying to get people to deliver the ideas that we've had in the most effective way, are too numerous to count but we couldn't have done it without them.

We'd also like to thank the contributors to our research, especially our experts who came forth with some insight into their own communication challenges and shared their wisdom.

With this book, we obviously tapped into something that resonated with others as they were all more than willing to share their thoughts and experiences on the challenges of communication in software development.

Thank you all for not keeping it to yourself.

If you have anything that you want to share with us in relation to the topics covered in this book then don't keep it to yourself, send us an email a info@dontkeepittoyourself.co.uk so we know what you're thinking.

Further reading or listening

Jeff Sutherland, The Art of Doing Twice the Work in Half the Time

David Baddiel Tries to Understand, BBC Podcasts

Richard Parks, Beyond the horizon

Valerie Young, The Secret Thoughts of Successful Women: Why Capable People Suffer From the Imposter Syndrome and How to Thrive in Spite of It

About the authors

Robert Drury

Rob has been working in and with software development teams since the turn of the century, with experience across recruitment, fundraising, ecommerce and finance products. He's worked for a number of digital agencies and more recently has been heading up the product functions in start-ups based in London. Rob is a regular contributor of business articles to Medium, Real Business, and Business Advice, and is a mentor for Brightside.org.uk, as well as being a father of five girls.

Stuart Dawson

Stuart started programming at a young age when his Dad bought him a programming book for the Acorn Electron. He sat down with it and attempted to write his own version of Donkey Kong. Although it didn't go quite to plan, he was not deterred. Following this he studied software engineering and has spent the last 22 years developing or delivering software in one guise or another, across a variety of industries and different tech stacks. Stuart is founder of The London Public Speaking for Software Engineers Meetup and regularly runs workshops to help others overcome the fear of public speaking.

www.ingramcontent.com/pod-product-compliance
Lightning Source LLC
Chambersburg PA
CBHW082255220526
45469CB00009B/3021